RACE AND THE MEDIA IN MODERN AMERICA

BY DUCHESS HARRIS, JD, PHD

WITH TAMMY GAGNE

Core Library

An Imprint of Abdo Publishing
abdobooks.com

Cover image: When singer and actress Zendaya wore her hair in dreadlocks to the 2015 Academy Awards, a fashion reporter criticized her. The same reporter praised Kylie Jenner, who is white, for wearing a similar style.

abdobooks.com

Published by Abdo Publishing, a division of ABDO, PO Box 398166, Minneapolis, Minnesota 55439. Copyright © 2021 by Abdo Consulting Group, Inc. International copyrights reserved in all countries. No part of this book may be reproduced in any form without written permission from the publisher. Core Library™ is a trademark and logo of Abdo Publishing.

Printed in the United States of America, North Mankato, Minnesota
102020
012021

THIS BOOK CONTAINS
RECYCLED MATERIALS

Cover Photo: Chris Pizzello/Invision/AP/Shutterstock Images
Interior Photos: Jeff Greenberg/Universal Images Group/Getty Images, 4–5, 8; Jeff Roberson/ AP Images, 10–11; Santa Clara County Sheriff's Office/AP Images, 13; Red Line Editorial, 14; RW/ MediaPunch/IPX/AP Images, 16; Autograph Magazine, 18–19; Evan Agostini/Invision/AP Images, 21; Shutterstock Images, 23, 29, 35; Jeff Kravitz/FilmMagic/Getty Images, 26–27, 43; Jordan Strauss/ Invision/AP Images, 30; Lev Radin/Shutterstock Images, 32–33; Shane Keyser/Kansas City Star/ Tribune News Service/Getty Images, 37; Dan MacMedan/WireImage/Getty Images, 40

Editor: Katharine Hale
Series Designer: Sarah Taplin

Library of Congress Control Number: 2020944157

Publisher's Cataloging-in-Publication Data

Names: Harris, Duchess, author. | Gagne, Tammy, author.
Title: Race and the media in modern America / by Duchess Harris and Tammy Gagne
Description: Minneapolis, Minnesota : Abdo Publishing, 2021 | Series: Core library guide to racism in modern America | Includes online resources and index
Identifiers: ISBN 9781532194696 (lib. bdg.) | ISBN 9781644945124 (pbk.) | ISBN 9781098214210 (ebook)
Subjects: LCSH: Race relations in mass media--Juvenile literature. | Mass media--Juvenile literature. | Prejudices in mass media--Juvenile literature. | United States--History--Juvenile literature. | Race relations--Juvenile literature.
Classification: DDC 305.8--dc23

CONTENTS

Recovered

4

MISSING FROM
THE NEWS

Yaniya Carter went missing near Atlanta, Georgia, in 2017. She was 14. Yaniya's mother, Yevette, reported her daughter missing. She told the police that it wasn't like Yaniya to leave without telling anyone. Yevette thought that Yaniya was with 19-year-old Gregory Harris. Yevette had told her daughter she couldn't date Harris. He was an adult. Yaniya was a minor.

On the same day, Caitlyn Frisina went missing in Florida. Caitlyn was 17. She was

Missing persons reports are often handled differently depending on the missing person's race.

OTHER STORIES

Jayme Closs was 13 when Jake Patterson killed her parents and kidnapped her. The missing teen's story appeared frequently on national news. After 88 days in captivity, Jayme escaped. Patterson was sentenced to life in prison.

Two-year-old Arianna Fitts's story did not receive the same attention. Her mother was killed in 2016. Arianna had last been seen with a babysitter. In March 2020, Arianna was still missing, and police offered a $100,000 reward for information on the case. According to a CNN report, some experts think race is behind the differences in coverage. Arianna is Black, and Jayme is white.

also thought to be in a relationship with an adult. Police believed she was romantically linked to her soccer coach, Rian Rodriguez. He was 27. Fortunately, both girls were soon found safe. But the media had handled the two stories differently.

Caitlyn's story quickly spread across news channels. But Yaniya's story received much less attention. There were important differences in the cases. Rodriguez was much older than Harris. He was also an authority figure as a coach. But many people think race also played a role. Caitlyn is white. Yaniya is Black.

BLACK MISSING PERSONS IGNORED

Approximately 800,000 Americans go missing each year. Of those, about 60 percent are people of color. In 2018, 30 percent of missing persons were Black. Most of these cases were not covered in the news. Only approximately 20 percent of cases of missing Black people are covered at all. Coverage is more widespread when white people go missing.

PERSPECTIVES
RAISING AWARENESS

Natalie and Derrica Wilson created the Black and Missing Foundation. Its goal is to help the families of missing Black and Hispanic children. The Wilsons wanted to bring awareness to the problems these families face. Natalie explains, "There are so many families of color who are desperately searching for their missing loved one and they are just asking for just one second or a couple of seconds of media coverage and it can change the narrative for them."

Attention such as news reports and missing person alerts are critical for finding missing persons.

Spreading the word is key in locating a missing person. When a story receives little or no press, it becomes much harder to find the person. News stories encourage the public to watch for the missing person. A delay in getting the word out makes finding the person much less likely.

Missing person cases are just one example of how the media treats people of color differently than white people. Other stories are reported with biased language or viewpoints. Similar bias can be identified in movies, television shows, and even advertising.

STRAIGHT TO THE
SOURCE

Basheera Agyeman wrote in her college newspaper about the disappearance of a ten-year-old girl in Washington, DC:

> *The true concern that has emerged with this story is that when children of color disappear, authorities make the assumption that they are simply runaways or that, somehow, they have a hand in their own disappearance. This is in contrast to the amount of attention that white children are likely to receive when they go missing. This is manifested in whether law enforcement decides to send out . . . alerts for missing children of color and how much time media outlets are likely to spend covering their stories, if they pick up the stories at all.*

> Source: Basheera Agyeman. "Media Ignores African Americans Missing in US." *Daily Evergreen*, 4 Apr. 2017, dailyevergreen.com. Accessed 2 Sept. 2020.

WHAT'S THE BIG IDEA?

Take a close look at this passage. What connections does Agyeman make between media coverage and police work? What evidence does she use to support these connections?

BIASED STORYTELLING

The media often reports stories about people of color differently than stories about white people. This is often the case when a person of color is accused of a crime. In 2014 the nation was focused on Ferguson, Missouri. White police officer Darren Wilson shot and killed an 18-year-old Black teen after a struggle. His name was Michael Brown. As the news spread, many stories focused on negative parts of Brown's past.

News outlets used photos that made Michael Brown look intimidating instead of photos such as this one held by his father.

Less than a year later, a 19-year-old white man was charged with sexual assault in California. Brock Turner's story also spread quickly. But these stories were different. Many stories did not focus on negative things about Turner. Instead, they talked about Turner's record as a swimmer at Stanford University. They discussed his dreams of competing in the Olympics.

Most news stories about Turner included his yearbook photo. Stories about Brown used images that made

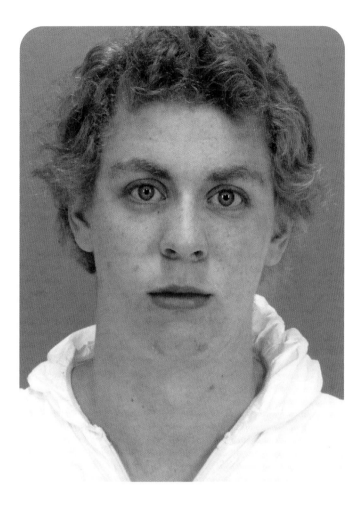

News outlets chose to show Brock Turner's yearbook photo rather than this mug shot or a court photo.

the Black teen look intimidating. Journalists routinely use mug shots in stories about Black people. But white people in similar stories are often shown in more positive photos.

This led to the hashtag #IfTheyGunnedMeDown. Many young Black people post this hashtag with

REPORTING
ON CRIME

Researchers studied the differences in crime reporting based on race. They studied news reports from January 2015 to December 2016. These graphs show the results. What do you notice about the graphs? How do the graphs help explain media bias?

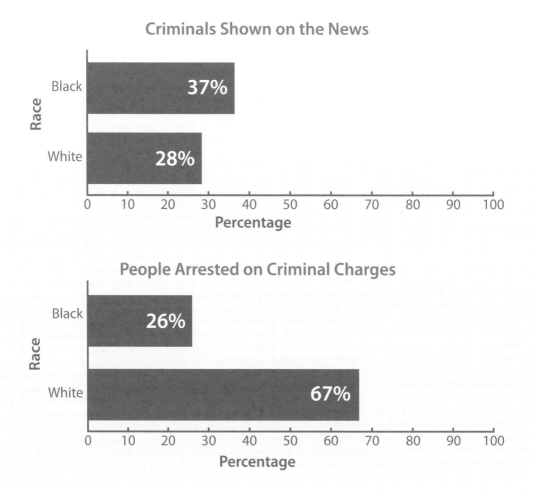

Criminals Shown on the News

Race	Percentage
Black	37%
White	28%

People Arrested on Criminal Charges

Race	Percentage
Black	26%
White	67%

two different photos of themselves. One shows a happy, positive moment. The other is more negative. The hashtag asks which picture the media would use if these people were to be killed by police.

SLANTED PERSPECTIVES

The media can show racial bias when discussing criminal suspects of different backgrounds. Black or Muslim suspects are often called *thugs* or *terrorists*. But white suspects are often called *mentally ill*. Communications expert Cynthia Frisby notes that mentioning mental illness can be a way to remove some of the blame

JOURNALISM ITSELF LACKS DIVERSITY

Only 7 percent of the people who work in US newsrooms are Black. Even fewer Black people hold positions of power in the news industry. Between 2013 and 2017, only 6 percent of US news directors were Black. A news director decides which stories to tell. Many newsrooms seek to make diversity a bigger priority at all levels. The more diverse newsrooms are, the less likely that stories will be biased.

More diversity in newsrooms can help reduce biased reporting.

from the shooter. This description also contributes
to a stereotype that people with mental illness
are dangerous. Studies indicate that only a small
percentage of shootings are committed by people with
mental health problems.

Journalists may not intend to be biased. Sometimes implicit bias plays a role. Implicit bias refers to unconscious stereotypes about other people. It can cause a journalist to tell a story from a biased perspective. Journalists may not think of themselves as racist. But racism is wrong even when unintentional. A journalist's top priority should be to report the facts accurately and without bias.

FURTHER EVIDENCE

Chapter Two discusses implicit bias and ways the media treats people of color differently than it treats white people. What was one of this chapter's main points? What evidence is included to support this point? Watch the videos at the website below. Does the information on the website support this point? Does it present new evidence?

WHO, ME? BIASED?

abdocorelibrary.com/race-and-the-media

RACIAL STEREOTYPES IN ENTERTAINMENT

Hollywood, like other areas of society, has a long-established issue with prejudice and racism. Many movies have portrayed harmful stereotypes about people of color. Early Hollywood did not have many roles for people of color. Instead, movies would hire a white actor to play a character of a different race. Actors did this by using makeup to change their skin color and facial features. When an actor portrays a Black person, this

Actor Mickey Rooney, pictured in a 1945 publicity photo, wore prosthetics to play an Asian character in 1961's *Breakfast at Tiffany's*. The film is criticized for its racist stereotyping.

PERSPECTIVES

OUT WITH THE OLD

Many old movies contain racial stereotypes. In 2020 a movement worked to stop showing these movies on television. Many early films show Black people in submissive roles. Journalist Georgianna Lawton sees these works as damaging. "Hollywood and our wider society are quick to heap praise upon Black people for playing narrowly defined roles which reflect an ideally unequal world where minorities are not so self-assured," she wrote. She argued that it was time to stop promoting these stereotypes. But not everyone showed support for the idea. Some people felt that these films were simply products of their time.

is called blackface. When an actor portrays an Asian person, it is called yellowface. These portrayals overplayed stereotypes and are offensive.

In 1930, a film industry rule called the Hays Code came into effect. This rule banned films from showing anything considered illegal or immoral. At that time, marriage between people of different races was illegal in 30 states. The Hays Code banned showing interracial

Ghost in the Shell is a popular Japanese manga. When white actress Scarlett Johansson was cast in the lead role of the film adaptation, many accused the film of whitewashing.

couples in movies. Filmmakers could use the Hays Code to justify hiring only white actors.

Today, movies and TV shows still struggle with diversity. One current problem is called whitewashing. This is when characters of color are played by white actors. With whitewashing, an actor does not pretend to be the character's race. Instead the character is portrayed as white. This can happen in adaptations from books or comics. It can also happen when telling true stories.

Movies and television shows affect how viewers think about race. People may not know others of different races. They can assume that an on-screen representation is accurate or comical when it's not. Many movies and television shows still have racial stereotypes. Black characters are often poor. They may be single parents or involved in crime. Black men are shown as angry or intimidating. Black women are shown to be loud or rude.

Asian characters are often shown as refugees or overachievers. Native American characters

WORDS MATTER

Dialogue refers to words spoken by characters in a movie or show. These spoken words drive the story line. They also tell an audience a lot about the characters. In 2017 the University of Southern California published a study on dialogue. Researchers looked at more than 1,000 scripts. They found that Black characters used profanity the most. Hispanic characters talked the most about sexuality. This can add to stereotypes surrounding characters of color.

The role models young people see in movies can affect their self-esteem.

are highly spiritual. Many are limited to life on a reservation. Middle Eastern characters are often violent. Hispanic characters are written as villains. Many are portrayed as heavy drinkers. Hispanic characters who are presented positively are often shown as exceptions.

THE HARM OF STEREOTYPES

Characters of all races are being shown more in film and on television. But the quality of their representation leaves much to be desired. Stereotypes shown in film and movies, from a character's occupation to personality traits, can have negative effects on viewers of all ages and races.

Racial stereotypes in entertainment can also hurt a person's self-image. Studies have shown that Black boys' self-esteem drops the more television they watch. The same is true for both Black and white girls. But white boys' self-esteem rises as they watch more television. Experts think this is because white men are often portrayed in a positive way. They are the heroes of their stories, with good jobs and beautiful wives. Women and people of color are limited to lesser roles. They often portray villains, sidekicks, and victims. Black men are often criminalized. Intentional or not, children often find role models in entertainment. When stereotypes are used, many of those models can be damaging.

STRAIGHT TO THE
SOURCE

Jordan Walker-Pearlman is a filmmaker. He has enjoyed movies since he was child. But he always hated the racial stereotypes he saw in many classic films. In an opinion piece for the *Miami Herald*, he wrote:

> *It's important to understand that this isn't about blaming an earlier generation for views common in its day or asking artists to know what tomorrow's sensitivities might be.*
>
> *Those earlier characterizations of people of color in movies were not merely cases of harmless ignorance, but a form of cultural violence. They were consciously created to legitimize hateful attitudes and make acceptable levels of social oppression with full knowledge of their effect.*

Source: Jordan Walker-Pearlman. "Beyond #OscarsSoWhite, Hollywood Needs to Confront Historic Racism on the Big Screen." *Miami Herald*, 5 Feb. 2020, miamiherald.com. Accessed 2 Sept. 2020

BACK IT UP

The author is using evidence to support a point. Write a paragraph describing the point the author is making. Then write down two or three pieces of evidence the author uses to make the point.

REPRESENTATION IN ENTERTAINMENT

People of color are underrepresented in entertainment. More than 80 percent of the lead actors in the top films of 2017 were white. Movies that do focus on characters of color often limit them to racial experiences. For example, Black actors may be cast as enslaved people. When those are the only stories viewers see, it can lead them to make incorrect assumptions. They may think actors of color can only appear in roles related to race.

Actor Chadwick Boseman was admired for his portrayals of T'Challa in *Black Panther* and Black historical figures such as Jackie Robinson.

BLACK SUPERHEROES

Movies about superheroes are very popular. But until 2018, there hadn't been a hit movie about a family-friendly Black superhero. *Black Panther* started conversations in the film industry. The movie challenged stereotypes about Africa. The movie's success showed how much Black families wanted a superhero who looked like them. *Black Panther* smashed box office records. It earned more than $1 billion worldwide in less than one month.

Actor Chadwick Boseman played T'Challa, the Black Panther. Boseman also played important Black historical figures such as Jackie Robinson. Robinson was a famous Black major league baseball player. Boseman inspired many Black people of all ages. He died in August 2020 from colon cancer.

Some directors work to include characters of different races. However, there is often just one person of color in a cast. This is often called a token character. The role may exist simply to make the cast look more diverse. Adding one person of color to a show does not truly offer diversity. A token character usually is not crucial to the plot. Token characters are often stereotyped.

DIVERSITY IN DIRECTORS

657 Male Directors

👤 74 Black   👤 39 Asian   👤 27 Latino   👤 517 White or Other Ethnicity

47 Female Directors

👤 5 Black   👤 3 Asian   👤 1 Latina   👤 38 White or Other Ethnicity

Women in general are underrepresented as directors. The problem is even worse for women of color. This graphic shows information about the 704 directors of the 1,200 most successful films from 2007 to 2018. How does the graphic help you better understand the text?

LACK OF RECOGNITION

Even when people of color get good roles, the actors are often overlooked for awards. White actors have often made up the entire group of nominees. Writers, directors, and crew members of color are also

Cheryl Boone Isaacs was president of the Academy of Motion Pictures Arts and Sciences from 2013 to 2017. In 2016 she helped implement a plan to increase the diversity of the Academy by 2020.

often ignored for awards. This has been seen at the Academy Awards, the top awards for movies.

In 2016 a large group of actors, writers, and directors began protesting this problem. The Academy Awards had not nominated a single Black actor. It was the second year in a row. The group used the social media hashtag #OscarsSoWhite. Members boycotted the Academy Awards ceremony that year. Spike Lee, Jada Pinkett Smith, and Will Smith were some of the stars who took part.

Following the boycott, the Academy took action. In 2015 only 8 percent of the people who voted for its awards were people of color. By 2020 that number had doubled. But the Academy still has a long way to go. In 2020 it announced a new diversity plan. Starting in 2024, movies would have to meet inclusion standards to be considered for the Best Picture award. Films would need to have people from underrepresented groups in the cast and crew. This includes racial and ethnic groups. The Academy hopes this will increase diversity.

PERSPECTIVES

THE DECISION MAKERS

Representation is an important step toward solving the diversity problem in movies. Many Academy members have said too few diverse films are being made. Almost all the decision makers within movie studios are white. Journalist David Cox wrote an article for the *Guardian* about this issue. "It is not the Academy that is cheating minorities, it is the film industry itself," he said. "Currently, ethnic minorities make up around 40 percent of America's population, yet they are outnumbered two to one among film leads, two to one among directors, and three to one among film writers."

RACE AND BRANDING

Race is an issue in many companies' branding. Branding involves names, logos, and mascots used to sell products. People have asked brands to change racist names and mascots for years. Aunt Jemima syrup and Uncle Ben's rice are two of these brands. These characters are based on Black stereotypes. In 2020 there were widespread protests for racial justice. As a result, the companies that own these two brands decided to make changes.

In 2020 Uncle Ben's rice announced it would change its name to Ben's Original and remove its mascot.

It is not only Black characters that are used in this way. Eskimo Pie has been making its ice cream products since 1921. The name of this product is offensive to people of Inuit and Yupik heritage. The word *Eskimo* was first used by white settlers in the Arctic region. It is an insulting term for the Native peoples there. In 2020 the company announced that it would be changing its name to Edy's Pie for this reason.

Land O'Lakes makes butter and other dairy products. The company had long featured a Native American woman on its packaging. The Land O'Lakes mascot is named Mia. She was designed by Ojibwe artist Patrick DesJarlait. Some people see nothing wrong with using the image. This includes the artist's son. Robert DesJarlait said that his father drew Mia as an Ojibwe woman. He says she is not a stereotype. However, because the company is not owned by Native Americans, the use of an Ojibwe woman's likeness is considered cultural appropriation. This is the act of taking things from other cultures and using them in a

Mia, the Land O'Lakes mascot, was designed by Ojibwe artist Patrick DesJarlait.

way that does not benefit those cultures. The company removed the image from its packaging in 2020.

THE PROBLEM WITH SPORTS TEAMS

Branding goes beyond products in grocery stores. Racial branding has long been used in the world of sports. Team names have been criticized as insulting to Native Americans. These include the Cleveland Indians

PERSPECTIVES

OUTSIDE PRESSURE

The decision to change a team's name is up to the owners. But related businesses can often play an important role. This was the case with the Washington, DC, football team. Three large companies put financial pressure on the team. Amazon announced that it would stop selling the team's merchandise. Pepsi threatened to pull its sponsorship. And FedEx said it would withdraw its sponsorship of the team's stadium. When the owners moved to change the name, the businesses agreed to keep working with them. Pepsi issued a statement of support. "We believe it is time for a change. We are pleased to see the steps the team announced today."

and the Washington Redskins. The name of the Washington football team is a racial slur. The Not Your Mascot movement works to educate people about the harm Native mascots cause. Protesters for the movement often shout, "We are a people, not your mascot."

After decades of pressure, Washington agreed to change its name in 2020. Cleveland began a formal name review. But owners of the

The Kansas City Chiefs' tomahawk chop, where fans move their arms down in a slicing motion, appropriates and disrespects Native American cultures.

Kansas City Chiefs, Atlanta Braves, and Chicago Blackhawks reacted differently. They think that their team names honor Native Americans. In 2020 they had no plans to change them. But other factors besides the names are offensive. For example, some fans show up with their faces painted red. Others buy toy tomahawks at the stadiums. They chant pretend war cries as they wave the toys in the air during games.

GOOD INTENTIONS GONE BAD

Companies throughout the world have issued press releases or statements that condemn racial injustices and promote equality. But sometimes their actions show a lack of true understanding of what people of color are up against. A 2017 Pepsi commercial featuring Kendall Jenner is one example. The ad shows Jenner joining a protest. The cause of the protest is not made clear. But many viewers thought it mirrored ongoing protests for racial equality. Jenner hands a police officer a can

MORE THAN WORDS

Many companies issued statements against racism in 2020. Activists asked them to do more. They asked companies to share information about their own diversity. Speaking out against racism is important. But hiring people of color, paying them well, and promoting them to leadership positions are more important. These steps make a bigger difference in the fight against racial inequality.

of Pepsi. This changes the entire mood of the group. Both the officer and the protesters begin smiling. The protesters cheer after the officer takes a sip.

Many viewers felt that Pepsi was making the issue of racial equality seem trivial. The ad suggested the problem could be solved with a drink. Pepsi later apologized. The company said it had been trying to promote "unity, peace and understanding." But critics of the ad felt it missed the mark.

SIGNS OF PROGRESS

Many companies have taken stands against racism in their advertising. A large number have issued public statements denouncing racism. Others have taken bigger steps, such as name or logo changes. Some have donated to organizations such as Black Lives Matter. This organization fights for racial equality.

Protests for racial equality in 2020 encouraged change. Media sources took a closer look at racial representation. More stories about race were being

William Jackson Harper played Chidi Anagonye on *The Good Place*. He was one of five Black actors nominated for Outstanding Supporting Actor in a Comedy at the 2020 Emmy awards.

reported on the news. And more people of color were being recognized in entertainment. In 2020 more Black artists were nominated for Emmys than in any previous year. The Emmys are the top awards for television. Singer and actress Zendaya made history at the

2020 Emmys. She became the youngest person to win Outstanding Lead Actress in a Drama.

Many films with whitewashing face backlash. People criticize the films. They do not watch them. This means the movies do not make as much money. Studios may make different casting decisions in the future.

Racism in the media may seem less important than biases people face in everyday life. But representation can have a big impact. Greater diversity in the media can help reduce underlying racism.

EXPLORE ONLINE

Chapter Five discusses racist branding. Read the article at the website below. How is the information from the article the same as the information in Chapter Five? What new information did you learn from the article?

TRADER JOE'S WORKING TO REMOVE PRODUCT BRANDING CRITICIZED AS RACIST

abdocorelibrary.com/race-and-the-media

IMPORTANT DATES

2014
Michael Brown is fatally shot by Ferguson police officer Darren Wilson. Many news reports focus on negative aspects of Brown's past. The hashtag #IfTheyGunnedMeDown begins spreading on social media.

2015
Brock Turner is arrested and charged with sexual assault. Many news reports focus on his accomplishments as a competitive swimmer at a prestigious college rather than his crime.

2016
Numerous celebrities boycott the Academy Awards when no Black actors are nominated for major awards for a second year.

2017
Teens Yaniya Carter and Caitlyn Frisina go missing the same day. The two cases are handled differently by the media.

2018
Black Panther is released and becomes a worldwide hit.

2020
Under great pressure, several companies and sports teams decide to change their branding to be more respectful to people of color. More Black artists receive Emmy nominations than in any previous year. The Academy announces new diversity requirements for Best Picture nominees.

Take a Stand

Robert DesJarlait was disappointed when Land O'Lakes removed Mia, its mascot, from its packaging. DesJarlait said his father drew Mia to reflect his Ojibwe heritage. Do you agree with DesJarlait? Or do you agree with Land O'Lakes that its logo needed to change? Why?

Dig Deeper

After reading this book, what questions do you still have about race and the media? With an adult's help, find a few reliable sources that can help you answer your questions. Write a paragraph about what you learned.

Tell the Tale

Chapter Two of this book discusses biased reporting. Imagine that you are a news reporter, and your job is to describe a crime that has been committed. How can you make sure you are using unbiased language in your report? Write 200 words about the steps you can take.

GLOSSARY

biased
prejudiced against someone
or something

boycott
to choose not to purchase
something or attend an
event as a protest

implicit bias
an unfair attitude toward
a person or group without
conscious knowledge

minor
a person under 18

mug shot
a photograph taken when a
person is arrested

reservation
land set aside for a Native
American tribe, often smaller
than its traditional lands

stereotype
an oversimplified
representation of a person
or group

tomahawk
a lightweight ax traditionally
used by many Native
American tribes

ONLINE RESOURCES

To learn more about race and the media, visit our free resource websites below.

Visit **abdocorelibrary.com** or scan this QR code for free Common Core resources for teachers and students, including vetted activities, multimedia, and booklinks, for deeper subject comprehension.

Visit **abdobooklinks.com** or scan this QR code for free additional online weblinks for further learning. These links are routinely monitored and updated to provide the most current information available.

LEARN MORE

Harris, Duchess. *Black Lives Matter*. Abdo Publishing, 2018.

Harris, Duchess, and Rebecca Rowell. *Hidden Heroes: The Human Computers of NASA*. Abdo Publishing, 2019.

ABOUT THE AUTHORS

Duchess Harris, JD, PhD

Dr. Harris is a professor of American Studies and Political Science at Macalester College and curator of the Duchess Harris Collection of ABDO books. She is also the coauthor of the collection, which features popular titles such as *Hidden Human Computers: The Black Women of NASA* and series including Freedom's Promise and Race and American Law. In addition, Dr. Harris hosts the *Freedom's Promise* podcast with her son.

Before working with ABDO, Dr. Harris authored several other books on the topics of race, culture, and American history. She served as an associate editor for *Litigation News*, the American Bar Association Section of Litigation's quarterly flagship publication, and was the first editor in chief of *Law Raza*, an interactive online journal covering race and the law, published at William Mitchell College of Law. She has earned a BA in History from the University of Pennsylvania, a PhD in American Studies from the University of Minnesota, and a JD from William Mitchell College of Law.

Tammy Gagne

Tammy Gagne has written dozens of books for both adults and children. Her recent titles include *The History of Racism in America* and *Justice for George Floyd*. She lives in northern New England with her husband and son.

INDEX